Math Strategies
A Problem-Solver's Journal

Student Book

Author
Mary Rosenberg

Project Manager
Marcia Russell, M.A. Ed.

Editors
Gisela Lee, M.A.
Jodene Smith, M.A.

Editor-in-Chief
Sharon Coan, M.S. Ed.

Product Director
Phil Garcia

Illustrator
Neri Garcia

Teacher Created Materials, Inc.
5301 Oceanus Drive
Huntington Beach, CA 92649
www.teachercreatedmaterials.com
ISBN-0-7439-0105-3
©2005 Teacher Created Materials, Inc.
Made in U.S.A.

Reprinted, 2006

Table of Contents

Introduction

Many students would agree that solving problems is one of the most difficult math skills to master. This book provides you with a variety of problems and a set of strategies to help solve them.

What is a strategy?

A strategy is a specific plan of action that has been carefully worked out. When you use a strategy correctly to help you understand and work through the steps of a problem, you become a better problem solver!

There are 7 strategies in this book.

1. **Drawing a Diagram**
2. **Drawing a Table**
3. **Acting It Out or Using Concrete Materials**
4. **Guessing and Checking**
5. **Creating an Organized List**
6. **Looking for a Pattern**
7. **Using Simpler Numbers**

Each strategy has a set of problem pages to solve using the strategy. You may not complete all of the strategies or solve every problem in this book. Your teacher will introduce some or all of the strategies and give you opportunities to practice using them to solve certain problems.

The Math Problems

Each problem page contains only one problem. You will be asked to use a specific strategy, to show your work, and to state your solution on the journal page. When you have completed a problem, your teacher may review the problem and solution with the class, or you may self-correct the page using an answer key with "sample strategies and solutions" to the problems.

Testing Your Progress

The last section of this book (Problem-Solving Strategy Test, page 85) includes a ten-problem test to see how well you can apply the strategies used in this book. Your teacher will let you know how many problems to solve and how the strategies are to be used.

The Solution to Problem Solving

Whether you are writing a story, answering questions on a test, or planning a party, you have to understand the task and make a plan before you actually "get to work." Solving mathematics problems is very much the same! It is important to choose a carefully thought-out plan of action, or *strategy*, for solving a problem. Following these four steps will help you tackle any math word problem.

❏ Step 1: Understanding the Problem

Read the problem carefully a number of times until you fully understand what it is about. You may need to discuss the problem with someone else or rewrite it in your own words.

Ask yourself questions such as, "What is the problem asking me to do? What information do I need to know to solve the problem?" Choose the information you know and decide what is unknown or needs to be discovered. Check for unnecessary information that can be confusing.

❏ Step 2: Planning and Communicating a Solution

Ask yourself, "How will I solve this problem?" Think about the different strategies that could be used. You could try to make predictions, or guesses, about the problem. Often these guesses guide you toward finding the solution.

Think about how this problem is similar to other problems you have solved. Use strategies like drawing a diagram or table, making an organized list, or looking for a pattern in the problem.

Write down ideas as you work so you don't forget the steps you used to solve the problem. Look over your ideas. Do they make sense? Will they help you find the solution? If you are having difficulty, reread the problem and rethink your strategy. Perhaps you should try another strategy. Remember that there can be more than one way to find the solution to a problem.

❏ Step 3: Reflecting and Generalizing

Think about whether the solution makes sense and if it has answered what was asked.

Draw or write down what you were thinking as you solved the problem. This gives you time to reflect, or think back, on your work. Explain the solution and the strategies you used to others. By discussing the problem and solution with someone else, you check your work and have the opportunity to share it with others.

❏ Step 4: Extension

Once you have reflected, or looked back at your work, take a step forward to see if you can come up with a new problem. Ask yourself "what if" questions that help you think about writing another problem that could be linked to your problem. "What if three people shared the winning ticket instead of two?" "What if Mr. Todd worked fifty hours a week rather than 40 hours?"

Drawing a Diagram

Drawing a diagram or picture of a word problem often helps you "see" the problem more clearly.

You can draw a diagram using simple symbols or pictures. Drawing diagrams also helps you keep track of the information in problems that have more than one step.

Before you begin using this strategy, you will learn about how and when to use diagrams to solve problems. Use the problems on the following pages to practice the strategy.

Today's Problem

Strategy: Drawing a Diagram

Problem

Brett made a seven-layer dip. In a bowl, Brett used guacamole for the bottom layer and ranch dressing for the top layer. The salsa was below the beans but on top of the cream cheese. The cheddar cheese was on top of the beans but below the ranch dressing. The hot sauce was on top of the guacamole but below the other five ingredients. In what order did Brett layer the ingredients?

Using the Strategy

My Solution

Today's Problem ②

Strategy: Drawing a Diagram

Problem

Four friends live in the Tall Towers Apartment building. The building is four stories high and has four apartments on each floor. Draw a diagram to show where each of the friends live.

1. Jim lives on the 4th floor in the apartment second from the left.
2. Robin lives down three floors from Jim and over one apartment to the left.
3. Billy lives two floors above Robin and over three apartments to the right.
4. Cheryl lives two floors below Jim and in the first apartment to the left of Billy's.

Using the Strategy

My Solution

Today's Problem

③

Strategy: Drawing a Diagram

Problem

Write the directions for going from Nancy's house to Warren's house.

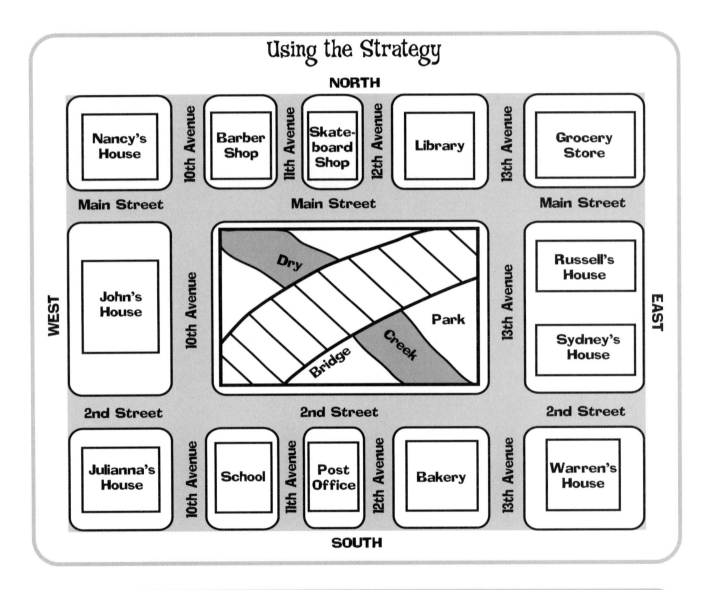

My Solution

Today's Problem

Strategy: Drawing a Diagram

Problem

Nicholas made a 9" x 12" cake. He cut the cake into 3" squares. How many pieces of cake are there?

Using the Strategy

My Solution

Today's Problem

Strategy: Drawing a Diagram

Problem

On a pegboard, Beth made a square 5 pegs by 5 pegs. She made a smaller square inside of it. What are the measurements of the smaller square? How many pegs are inside the smaller square?

Using the Strategy

My Solution

Today's Problem

Strategy: Drawing a Diagram

Problem

Below are sections from a hundreds board. Write the missing numbers in the empty spaces.

Using the Strategy

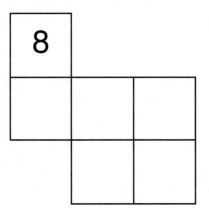

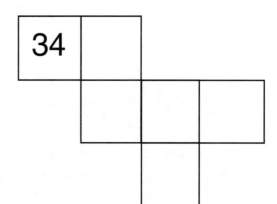

My Solution

Today's Problem

Strategy: Drawing a Diagram

Problem

Make a number line. Plot the following numbers on the number line.

876, 11, 728, 565, 240, 57, 142, 169, 912, 32

Using the Strategy

My Solution

12

Today's Problem

Strategy: Drawing a Diagram

Problem

The garden wall is 14" high. A snail crawls up 3" and slides down 1" every three minutes. How long will it take the snail to reach the top of the wall?

Using the Strategy

My Solution

Today's Problem

Strategy: Drawing a Diagram

Problem

Giselle is at the Fun Park.

From the Ticket Booth to the Fun House, she has to walk two blocks. It is twice as far from the Fun House to the House of Mirrors.

From the House of Mirrors to the Roller Mountain, Giselle has to walk three blocks. Giselle has to walk twice as far from Roller Mountain back to the Ticket Booth.

How far does Giselle walk in all?

Using the Strategy

My Solution

Today's Problem

Strategy: Drawing a Diagram

Problem

Steve needs to divide a candy bar equally among six friends. How many straight cuts does Steve need to make? If Steve wanted to divide the candy bar among nine friends, how many straight cuts would he need to make?

Using the Strategy

My Solution

Today's Problem

Strategy: Drawing a Diagram

Problem

Jason has a baseball, basketball, football, and volleyball arranged on a shelf in his bedroom.

The volleyball is between the baseball and the basketball.

The baseball is in between the football and the volleyball.

The basketball is not first.

What is the final order of the balls on the shelf?

Using the Strategy

My Solution

Today's Problem (12)

Strategy: Drawing a Diagram

Problem

There are four of each of the following kinds of trees: pear, orange, cherry, and apple. The trees are planted in four rows with four trees in each row. There cannot be more than two of the same tree in each row, column, and diagonal.

How could the trees be planted?

Is it possible to have only one of each tree in the same row, column, and diagonal?

Using the Strategy

My Solution

Drawing a Table

When a problem has lots of information, placing the information in a table is a good idea. A table helps you organize the information so that it can be easily understood.

A table makes it easy to see what information is there and what information is missing. When a table is drawn, the information often shows a pattern, or part of a solution, which can then be completed.

You will usually have to create some of the information in order to complete the table and then solve the problem.

Using a table can help reduce the chance of making mistakes or repeating something.

It is not always easy to decide how to divide up the information in the problem or make a table that works with the information. With practice, you will learn how to use a table to solve problems.

Before you begin using this strategy, you will learn about how and when to use tables to solve problems. Use the problems on the following pages to practice the strategy.

Today's Problem

Strategy: Drawing a Table

Problem

Mr. Robot computes three multiplication problems for every five addition problems and every four subtraction problems. If Mr. Robot has computed 20 subtraction problems, how many multiplication and addition problems have been computed?

Using the Strategy

My Solution

Today's Problem

Strategy: Drawing a Table

Problem

In a class of 20, there are two girls for every three boys. How many boys and girls are in the class?

Using the Strategy

My Solution

20

Today's Problem

Strategy: Drawing a Table

Problem

Laura sells three strawberry pies for every four lemon pies. If Laura sells 15 strawberry pies, how many lemon pies will have been sold? How many pies were sold in all?

Using the Strategy

My Solution

Today's Problem

Strategy: Drawing a Table

Problem

Write the rule for each table.

Using the Strategy

A.

23	17
85	79
63	57
90	84

B.

33	23
92	82
42	32
49	39

C.

43	33
16	6
41	31
29	19

D.

23	16
82	75
51	44
78	71

My Solution

Today's Problem (17)

Strategy: Drawing a Table

Problem

Complete each table.

Here's an example.

# In	# Out
4	3
3	2
8	7
6	5
5	4

Using the Strategy

A.

# In	# Out
4	5
0	
10	
9	
1	

B.

# In	# Out
8	10
11	
4	
7	
0	

C.

# In	# Out
6	4
2	
9	
7	
12	

My Solution

Today's Problem

Strategy: Drawing a Table

Problem

Complete each table. Write the rule.

Using the Strategy

A.

28	38
	96
19	29
	32

B.

48	
18	8
28	
	17

C.

411	401
929	
663	653
	725

D.

637	647
953	
303	313
	119

My Solution

Strategy: Drawing a Table

Problem

There are an equal number of chickens and sheep on a farm. There are 30 legs in all. How many chickens and sheep are there?

Using the Strategy

My Solution

Today's Problem

Strategy: Drawing a Table

Problem

Amy earns 10 cents for each paper she delivers. She puts 3 cents in her piggy bank and spends the rest. If Amy delivers ten papers, how much money does she earn, save, and spend?

Using the Strategy

My Solution

Today's Problem

Strategy: Drawing a Table

Problem

Every day the Wilsons put money into the family's piggy bank. Dad puts in 10 cents. Mom puts in 15 cents. Junior puts in 5 cents. How much money is in the piggy bank at the end of one week? How much money does each family member put in the piggy bank?

Using the Strategy

My Solution

Today's Problem

Strategy: Drawing a Table

Problem

Doug goes to the gym every Monday, Wednesday, and Friday. Spencer goes every fourth day beginning on the first day of the month. How many times this month will Doug and Spencer both be at the gym on the same day?

Using the Strategy

June

Sunday	Monday	Tuesday	Wednesday	Thursday	Friday	Saturday
		1	2	3	4	5
6	7	8	9	10	11	12
13	14	15	16	17	18	19
20	21	22	23	24	25	26
27	28	29	30			

My Solution

Acting It Out or Using Concrete Materials

Using objects, or materials such as counters and blocks, to represent people, places, or things in a problem often helps you find a solution more easily.

These objects can be moved through the steps of the problem. By showing this movement, you keep track of what is happening as you solve the problem.

It can also be helpful to act out the roles of the different people or objects in the problem. Building a model will sometimes clarify questions in the problem.

Before you begin using this strategy, you will learn about how and when to act out a problem or use concrete materials to solve problems. Use the problems on the following pages to practice the strategy.

Today's Problem

Strategy: Acting It Out or Using Concrete Materials

Problem

Five blocks have each been labeled with one of these letters—H, I, J, K, L. The H block is immediately to the right of the I block. The J block is to the right of the K block. The H is between the I and K. The L is immediately to the left of the I. Where is the J?

Using the Strategy

My Solution

Today's Problem (24)

Strategy: Acting It Out or Using Concrete Materials

Problem

Carrie and Bill are standing back to back. Each moves six steps forward, turns right and moves six steps forward. They then turn right again and move six steps forward. Finally, they turn right once more and move six steps forward. Where are Carrie and Bill now? (Hint: Plot the steps out on the graph paper below.)

Using the Strategy

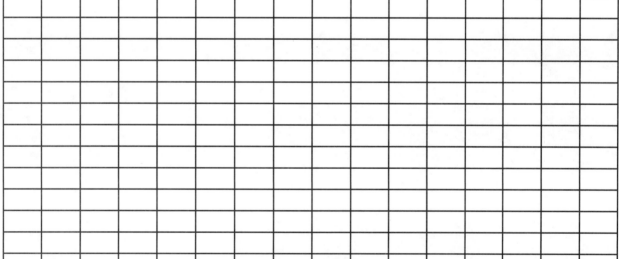

My Solution

Today's Problem

Strategy: Acting It Out or Using Concrete Materials

Problem

There were 40 cookies on the assembly line. Starting with the 7th cookie, Bobby tasted every 6th one. How many cookies did Bobby taste?

Using the Strategy

My Solution

Today's Problem

Strategy: Acting It Out or Using Concrete Materials

Problem

There are three bowls. In each bowl there are some blocks. There are five more blocks in the second bowl than in the first bowl. There are five more blocks in the third bowl than in the second bowl. There are 21 blocks in all. How many blocks are in each bowl?

Using the Strategy

My Solution

Today's Problem

Strategy: Acting It Out or Using Concrete Materials

Problem

Paul has a licorice rope that is 48" long. He gives a 9" length to Ruby, an 8" length to Mike, and 10" lengths to both Shelby and Henry. How long is Paul's licorice rope now?

Using the Strategy

My Solution

Today's Problem

Strategy: Acting It Out or Using Concrete Materials

Problem

Jason has a bowl filled with 20 blue counters. Jason takes out nine blue counters and puts in six red counters. Then he takes out seven blue counters and puts in seven red counters. Then he takes out two blue counters and puts in eight red counters. How many blue counters are in the bowl? How many red counters are in the bowl? How many counters in all?

Using the Strategy

My Solution

Today's Problem

Strategy: Acting It Out or Using Concrete Materials

Problem

Jasmine has an 8" square piece of paper. She cuts the paper in half. She takes one of the halves and cuts it in half. She does this three more times. How many pieces of paper does Jasmine now have?

Using the Strategy

My Solution

Today's Problem

Strategy: Acting It Out or Using Concrete Materials

Problem

Jonah had a $20 bill. He exchanged the bill for two $10 bills. He took one of the $10 bills and exchanged it for two $5 bills. He took one of the $5 bills and exchanged it for five $1 bills. Jonah took a $1 bill and exchanged it for four quarters. What bills and coins does Jonah now have?

Using the Strategy

My Solution

Today's Problem

Strategy: Acting It Out or Using Concrete Materials

Problem

There are ten cups in a line.

A penny is placed in every second cup.

A nickel is placed in every third cup.

A dime is placed in every fourth cup.

A quarter is placed in every fifth cup.

Which cup has the most money inside of it?

Using the Strategy

My Solution

Today's Problem

Strategy: Acting It Out or Using Concrete Materials

Problem

Dinah has six green marbles. She trades three of the green marbles for two orange marbles. She then trades one orange marble and one green marble for two blue marbles. Dinah trades one orange marble for two yellow marbles. Dinah finally trades one marble of each color for one cat's eye marble. How many marbles does Dinah now have? How many marbles of each kind or color does Dinah now have?

Using the Strategy

My Solution

Today's Problem

Strategy: Acting It Out or Using Concrete Materials

Problem

There are twelve bottles in a row. The bottles are numbered 1 to 12. Cora removes every 5th bottle. Out of the remaining bottles, John removes every 3rd bottle. Then Sandy removes every 6th bottle. Hank follows by removing every 2nd bottle. Shirley removes the remaining bottles. Which numbered bottles does Shirley remove?

Using the Strategy

My Solution

Guessing and Checking

Guessing and checking can be used to solve a variety of problems. Begin with an educated guess (a guess based on information you already know or ideas that seem reasonable). Don't make a wild guess.

Base your first guess on important facts. Check your guess against the facts and information in the problem.

If your guess is wrong, change it according to whether it is too small or too large.

Repeat these steps until you find the solution.

Learning how to make reasonable guesses will take practice. The best way to work with the facts in the problem is to draw a table.

The table helps you keep track of your guesses and results (checks) until you find the correct solution.

Before you begin using this strategy, you will learn about how and when to use "guess and check" to solve problems. Use the problems on the following pages to practice the strategy.

Today's Problem

Strategy: Guessing and Checking

Problem

Arrange the numbers 5, 6, 7, 8, 9, and 10 so that all three sides of the triangle equal 21.

Using the Strategy

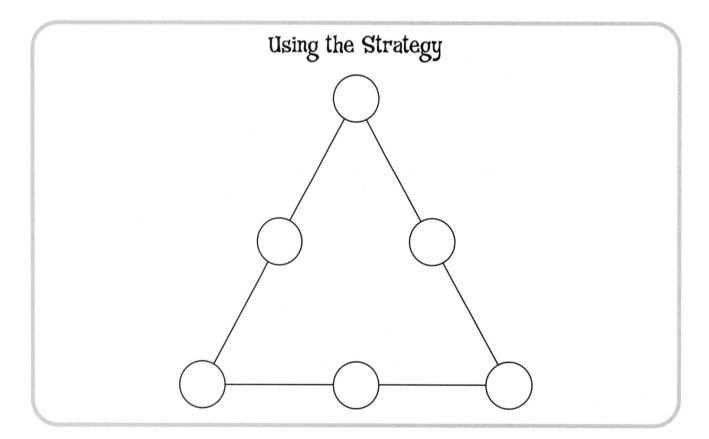

My Solution

Today's Problem

Strategy: Guessing and Checking

Problem

Use the numbers 4, 5, 6, 7, 8, 9, 10, 11, and 12 to complete the Magic Square. All rows and columns must equal 24. Each number may only be used one time.

Using the Strategy

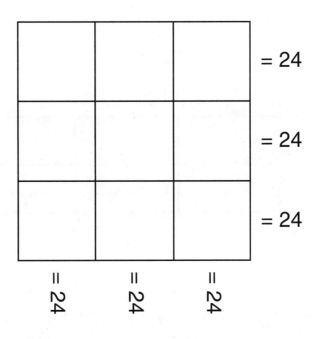

My Solution

Today's Problem

Strategy: Guessing and Checking

Problem

Simon sees some spiders and ladybugs. He sees 40 legs in all. How many spiders and ladybugs did Simon see?

Using the Strategy

Guess	1	2	3	4	5
Spiders					
Ladybugs					
Total					

My Solution

Today's Problem

Strategy: Guessing and Checking

Problem

The Jones kids' ages total 33 years. Sue is twice as old as Bill and three times older than Todd. How old are Sue, Bill, and Todd?

Using the Strategy

My Solution

Today's Problem

Strategy: Guessing and Checking

Problem

Jane has $1.00 in nickels, dimes, and quarters. She has more dimes than nickels and more nickels than quarters. How many of each coin does Jane have?

Using the Strategy

Guess	Number/Value	Number/Value	Number/Value	Number/Value
Nickels				
Dimes				
Quarters				
Total				

My Solution

Today's Problem

Strategy: Guessing and Checking

Problem

Brenda, Frank, and Stacy have a combined total of $5.00. Brenda has the most money and Stacy has the least amount of money. Everybody has at least $1.00 and nobody has more than $2.00. All money amounts are in increments of $0.25. How much money does each person have?

Using the Strategy

Guess	1	2	3	4	5
Brenda					
Frank					
Stacy					
Total					

My Solution

Today's Problem

Strategy: Guessing and Checking

Problem

Kate has $1.00 in pennies and dimes. She has 12 more pennies than dimes. How many pennies and dimes does Kate have?

Using the Strategy

My Solution

Today's Problem

Strategy: Guessing and Checking

Problem

David is thinking of a two-digit number. When the two digits are added together the sum is ten. When one digit is subtracted from the other, the difference is two. The digit in the tens place is larger than the digit in the ones place. What is David's mystery number?

Using the Strategy

My Solution

Creating an Organized List

Organizing information is a very important skill. You can use this skill to help solve problems.

When a problem has a large amount of information, it is sometimes best to organize it into a list. Then you can follow an order or sequence to find the solution.

Making an organized list is especially helpful when you need to decide how many ways a group of items can be combined.

When creating a list, one item usually stays the same while the others change.

Before you begin using this strategy, you will learn about how and when to create a list to solve problems. Use the problems on the following pages to practice the strategy.

Today's Problem

Strategy: Creating an Organized List

Problem

How many three-digit numbers can be made using the digits 1, 5, and 8? Order the numbers from smallest to greatest.

Using the Strategy

My Solution

Today's Problem

Strategy: Creating an Organized List

Problem

Use the digits 4, 5, 7, and 8 to make two 2-digit even numbers and two 2-digit odd numbers.

Add the two odd numbers. Is the sum odd or even?

Add the two even numbers. Is the sum odd or even?

Add an odd number and an even number. Is the sum odd or even?

Using the Strategy

My Solution

Today's Problem

Strategy: Creating an Organized List

Problem

A pair of dice is rolled. The two rolled numbers are then added together. How many different ways can you roll a total of 6?

Using the Strategy

My Solution

Today's Problem

Strategy: Creating an Organized List

Problem

Marisol has $18.00 to spend at the Tennis Pro Shop. She wants to buy three different items. Make a list showing the different combinations of three items that Marisol could buy without going over $18.00.

- tennis racquet $7.00
- water bottle $5.00
- tennis balls $3.00
- tennis bag $7.00
- tennis shoes $6.00
- tennis clothes $12.00

Using the Strategy

My Solution

Today's Problem

Strategy: Creating an Organized List

Problem

How many two-step addition and subtraction problems can be made using the numbers 6, 7, and 8? (Addition and subtraction must be used in the same problem.)

Using the Strategy

My Solution

Strategy: Creating an Organized List

Problem

Select 3 numbers to add to make an answer of 20. Each number can only be used one time. Make a list of the different ways to make 20. Hint: $9 + 7 + 4 = 20$, $9 + 4 + 7 = 20$, $7 + 9 + 4 = 20$, $7 + 4 + 9 = 20$, $4 + 7 + 9 = 20$, and $4 + 9 + 7 = 20$ and are all the same problem.

Using the Strategy

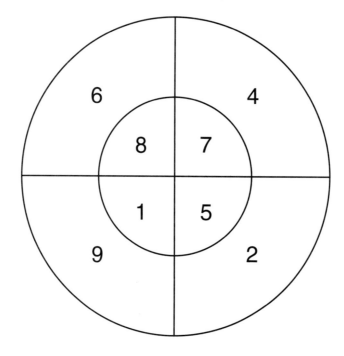

My Solution

Today's Problem

Strategy: Creating an Organized List

Problem

How many different multiplication problems can be made using the numbers 2, 3, 5, and 10?

Using the Strategy

My Solution

Today's Problem

Strategy: Creating an Organized List

Problem

How many different division problems can be made using the numbers 2, 4, 5, 10, and 20?

Using the Strategy

My Solution

Today's Problem 50

Strategy: Creating an Organized List

Problem

Each contestant gets to spin the wheel three times and earn the total dollar amount. What are the possible number of money combinations that a contestant could spin?

What is the largest amount of money that could be earned? What is the smallest amount of money that could be earned?

Using the Strategy

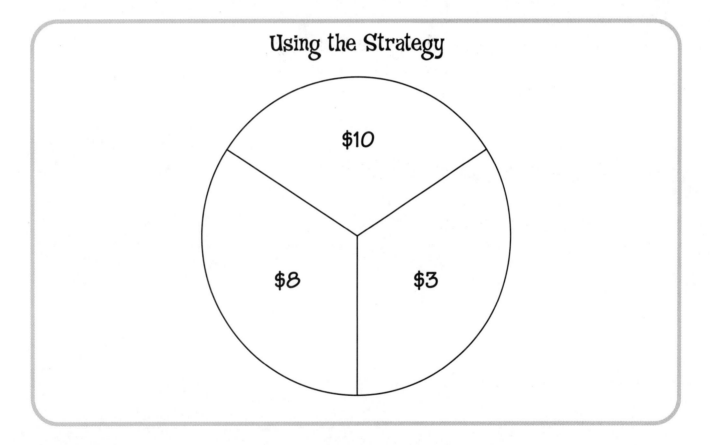

My Solution

Today's Problem

Strategy: Creating an Organized List

Problem

There are three desks in a row. How many different ways can Alex, Betty, and Carson be assigned to the desks?

Using the Strategy

My Solution

Today's Problem

Strategy: Creating an Organized List

Problem

Kendra wants a triple scoop of ice cream. Her ice cream choices are chocolate, vanilla, and strawberry. How many different combinations of ice cream does Kendra have to pick from? (Note: A cone of chocolate, vanilla, and strawberry is the same as a strawberry, chocolate and vanilla.)

Using the Strategy

My Solution

Today's Problem (53)

Strategy: Creating an Organized List

Problem

Natasha is designing her own wagon. She needs to pick a body color, a set of wheels, and a handle length. How many different cominations does Natasha have to choose from?

- *Body colors*: red or blue
- *Wheels*: black or white
- *Handles*: short or long

Using the Strategy

My Solution

Looking for a Pattern

Mathematical patterns can be found everywhere—in nature, in numbers, and in shapes. So, it is not surprising that the strategy of "Looking for a Pattern" is used often.

When you find a pattern, it becomes easy to predict what comes next.

You will find that the problem-solving strategies you learn are sometimes connected to one another. You may use more than one strategy to solve a problem. As you learn more about "Looking for a Pattern," you will find that it is often an extension of "Drawing a Table" or "Creating an Organized List."

Before you begin using this strategy, you will learn about how and when to look for a pattern to solve problems. Use the problems on the following pages to practice the strategy.

Today's Problem

Strategy: Looking for a Pattern

Problem

Color the numbers used when counting by 2s red.

Use an orange crayon to circle the numbers used when counting by 5s.

Put a blue X on the numbers used when counting by 10s.

Describe each skip counting pattern.

Using the Strategy

1	2	3	4	5	6	7	8	9	10
11	12	13	14	15	16	17	18	19	20
21	22	23	24	25	26	27	28	29	30
31	32	33	34	35	36	37	38	39	40
41	42	43	44	45	46	47	48	49	50
51	52	53	54	55	56	57	58	59	60
61	62	63	64	65	66	67	68	69	70
71	72	73	74	75	76	77	78	79	80
81	82	83	84	85	86	87	88	89	90
91	92	93	94	95	96	97	98	99	100

My Solution

64   ©Teacher Created Materials, Inc.

Today's Problem

Strategy: Looking for a Pattern

Problem

Extend each pattern. Write the rule.

Using the Strategy

65, 75, 85, _____, _____, _____, _____

189, 289, 389, _____, _____, _____, _____

413, 418, 423, _____, _____, _____, _____

My Solution

Today's Problem

Strategy: Looking for a Pattern

Problem

Complete the addition squares.

(**Hint:** You can only add up the squares going in one direction.)

Example

30	20	10
20	15	5
15	10	5

Using the Strategy

A.

		7
10	9	
	6	6

B.

13		
11	9	2
	9	4

My Solution

Strategy: Looking for a Pattern

Problem

Extend each pattern. Write the rule.

Using the Strategy

1, 2, 4, 8, _____, _____, _____, _____, _____

50, 49, 47, 44, _____, _____, _____, _____, _____

357, 360, 363, 366, _____, _____, _____, _____

474, 467, 460, 453, _____, _____, _____, _____

My Solution

Today's Problem

Strategy: Looking for a Pattern

Problem

Complete the number walls.

Example

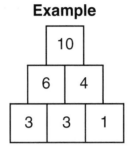

Using the Strategy

A.

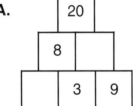

B.

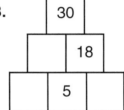

C.

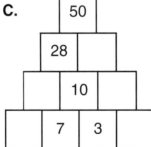

My Solution

Today's Problem

Strategy: Looking for a Pattern

Problem

Use a hundreds board to identify the missing numbers in the pattern.

Using the Strategy

1	2	3	4	5	6	7	8	9	10
11	12	13	14	15	16	17	18	19	20
21	22	(23)	24	25	26	27	28	29	30
31	(32)	33	34	35	36	37	38	39	40
41	42	(43)	44	45	46	47	48	49	50
51	(52)	53	54	55	56	57	58	59	60
61	62	(63)	64	65	66	67	68	69	70
71	(72)	73	74	75	76	77	78	79	80
81	82	(83)	84	85	86	87	88	89	90
91	(92)	93	94	95	96	97	98	99	100

My Solution

Today's Problem

Strategy: Looking for a Pattern

Problem

How many faces are on one cube?

If two cubes are put together, how many faces would there be?

If three cubes are put together, how many faces would there be?

If four cubes are put together, how many faces would there be?

Using the Strategy

My Solution

Today's Problem

Strategy: Looking for a Pattern

Problem

Use a circle, a square, and a triangle to make a repeating pattern. Use letters or numbers to label the pattern.

Using the Strategy

My Solution

Today's Problem

Strategy: Looking for a Pattern

Problem

Look for a pattern in this row of squares. Shade in the last three squares to finish the pattern.

Using the Strategy

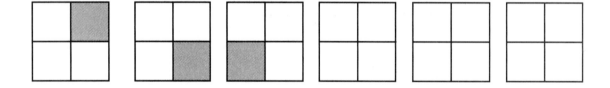

My Solution

Today's Problem

Strategy: Looking for a Pattern

Problem

Extend the pattern for each set of fractions.

Using the Strategy

$\dfrac{1}{2}$, $\dfrac{1}{3}$, $\dfrac{1}{4}$, $\dfrac{1}{5}$, _____, _____, _____, _____

$\dfrac{1}{1}$, $\dfrac{1}{2}$, $\dfrac{1}{4}$, $\dfrac{1}{8}$, _____, _____, _____, _____

$\dfrac{1}{2}$, $\dfrac{2}{4}$, $\dfrac{3}{6}$, $\dfrac{4}{8}$, _____, _____, _____, _____

My Solution

Today's Problem

Strategy: Looking for a Pattern

Problem

Extend the pattern. Write the rule.

Using the Strategy

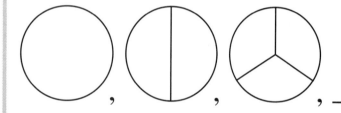

My Solution

Today's Problem

Strategy: Looking for a Pattern

Problem

Extend each pattern. Write the rule.

Using the Strategy

A. $.05, $.07, $.10, $.14, _____, _____, _____, _____

B. $.89, $.94, $.99, $1.04, _____, _____, _____, _____

C. $3.32, $3.40, $3.48, $3.56, _____, _____, _____, _____

My Solution

Using Simpler Numbers

What can you do if you come across a problem that seems too difficult to solve? If it has large numbers or complicated number concepts, you can use simpler numbers to help you understand what you need to do. Then, you'll be ready to tackle the hard problem!

Using simpler numbers can help in several ways. One way is that you will understand what operations you need to use to solve the problem. Try replacing the large numbers in the problem with smaller numbers. Then, solve the problem. If the answer makes sense for the smaller numbers, then you can use the same operations with the larger numbers.

Another way to use simpler numbers is to break down the problem into smaller parts. As you solve each part, keep track of your answers by drawing pictures or a table. Soon, you may see a pattern that will help you solve the big problem.

Before you begin using this strategy, you will learn when to use smaller numbers to solve a problem and how to break up a problem into parts to solve it. Use the problems on the following pages to practice the strategy.

Today's Problem 66

Strategy: Using Simpler Numbers

Problem

While counting cars, Joshua noticed there were five black cars for every three red cars and every two white cars. If 100 cars pass by, how many cars are black, red, and white?

Using the Strategy

My Solution

Today's Problem

Strategy: Using Simple Numbers

Problem

The Rounding Machine takes a number and rounds it to the nearest ten. Complete the table.

Using the Strategy

Rounding Machine

In	Out
84	80
96	100
74	
73	
67	
91	
22	
81	
66	
15	
88	
9	

My Solution

Today's Problem

Strategy: Using Simpler Numbers

Problem

Roz has 100 pennies. She gives half of the pennies to her friend, Todd. Todd gives half of his pennies to Mia. Mia gives five pennies to Stan and half of her remaining pennies to Roz. How many pennies does Roz now have?

Using the Strategy

My Solution

Today's Problem

Strategy: Using Simpler Numbers

Problem

At the Pet Shop there are 53 cats and dogs for sale. There are five more cats than dogs. How many dogs are there? How many cats are there?

Using the Strategy

My Solution

Today's Problem

Strategy: Using Simpler Numbers

Problem

Alexa is thinking of two consecutive numbers that when added together have a sum of 127. What are Alexa's two numbers?

Using the Strategy

My Solution

Today's Problem

Strategy: Using Simpler Numbers

Problem

Pick a number from Box B to subtract from Box A. Try to make subtraction problems with a difference between 40 and 80.

Using the Strategy

A

23	89
67	
45	90

B

	12
34	56
78	

My Solution

Today's Problem

Strategy: Using Simpler Numbers

Problem

There are a total of twelve tricycles, bicycles, and quadcycles at the local bike shop. There are a total of 40 wheels in all. How many of each kind of bike are at the shop?

Using the Strategy

My Solution

Notes

Choosing and Using the Strategies

Some or all of the following pages will be used to test how well you apply the strategies you learned in this book. Your teacher will let you know how many of the problems you should complete. He or she will also tell you whether you need to use certain strategies, or whether you can solve the problems by choosing from among any of the strategies in this book.

In the space provided on each page, write your name and the strategy (or strategies) you will use for that problem. Remember to show your work in the "Using the Strategy" section of each problem page and to write the solution in the "My Solution" section.

Name

Strategy:

Problem

For lunch, Larry has a sandwich, cookies, and fruit. How many different ways can Larry eat his lunch?

Using the Strategy

My Solution

Name

B

Strategy:

Problem

Jenny puts one penny in her piggy bank on Sunday, two pennies on Monday, four pennies on Tuesday, and eight pennies on Wednesday. If Jenny continues to put pennies in her piggy bank at this rate, how many pennies will she put into her piggy bank on Saturday? What will be the total amount of money in the piggy bank?

Using the Strategy

My Solution

Name

Strategy:

Problem

Arnold has 18 gumballs and jawbreakers. He has two more jawbreakers than gumballs. How many of each kind of candy does Arnold have?

Using the Strategy

My Solution

Name

D

Strategy:

Problem

Jacob is building a Lego® figure. It takes him one and a half seconds to join two pieces. How long will it take him to join nine pieces into one long strip?

Using the Strategy

My Solution

Name

Strategy: _____

Problem

Joanne has shirts in red, orange, and yellow. She has a green skirt, a pair of blue shorts, and a pair of purple jeans. How many different outfits can Joanne make?

Using the Strategy

My Solution

Name

Strategy:

Problem

At school four classmates say "Hello" to each other. How many times is "Hello" said?

Using the Strategy

My Solution

Name

Strategy: _____

Problem

Harriet has six shapes: circle, hexagon, pentagon, rectangle, square, and trapezoid. She arranges them in the following order.

1. None of the shapes with four sides are next to each other.
2. The hexagon is in between the square and the rectangle.
3. The circle is to the right of the rectangle.
4. The trapezoid is first.
5. The pentagon is between the trapezoid and the square.

Using the Strategy

My Solution

Name

H

Strategy:

Problem

At the Broom Factory, for every 6 brooms made, 2 are painted gold. How many brooms are painted gold if 36 brooms are made?

Using the Strategy

My Solution

Name

Strategy:

Problem

Find the common multiples for 2, 3, 4 to the 10th multiple.

Using the Strategy

My Solution

Name

Strategy:

Problem

Kathy makes a square out of blocks. Each side of the square is nine blocks long. How many blocks does Kathy use in all?

Using the Strategy

My Solution

Journal Reflection

On the lines provided, write about a strategy you learned as you worked on the problems in this journal. Explain the strategy and describe how, by applying it, you were able to solve a problem more easily. You may use a specific example if you wish.

_____

_____

_____

_____

_____

_____

_____

_____

_____

_____

_____

_____

_____

_____

_____

_____

_____

_____

_____

_____